ALSO BY RICHARD McGUIRE

HERE

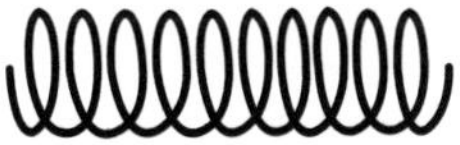

SEQUENTIAL DRAWINGS

THE NEW YORKER SERIES

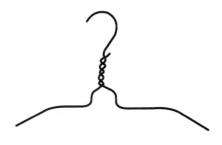

BY

RICHARD McGUIRE

HAMISH HAMILTON
an imprint of
PENGUIN BOOKS

HAMISH HAMILTON

UK | USA | CANADA | IRELAND | AUSTRALIA
INDIA | NEW ZEALAND | SOUTH AFRICA

HAMISH HAMILTON IS PART OF THE PENGUIN RANDOM HOUSE GROUP OF COMPANIES WHOSE ADDRESSES CAN BE FOUND AT GLOBAL.PENGUINRANDOMHOUSE.COM.

Penguin Random House UK

FIRST PUBLISHED IN THE UNITED STATES OF AMERICA BY PANTHEON BOOKS 2016
FIRST PUBLISHED IN THE UNITED KINGDOM BY HAMISH HAMILTON 2016
001

THE IMAGES IN THIS BOOK HAVE APPEARED, INDIVIDUALLY AND IN SLIGHTLY DIFFERENT FORM, IN THE *NEW YORKER* BETWEEN 2005 AND 2015

PRODUCTION DESIGN BY KATE RYAN

PRINTED IN GREAT BRITAIN BY CLAYS LTD, ST IVES PLC

A CIP CATALOGUE RECORD FOR THIS BOOK IS AVAILABLE FROM THE BRITISH LIBRARY
ISBN: 978-0-241-28752-1

www.greenpenguin.co.uk

FSC www.fsc.org MIX Paper from responsible sources FSC® C018179

Penguin Random House is committed to a sustainable future for our business, our readers and our planet. This book is made from Forest Stewardship Council® certified paper.

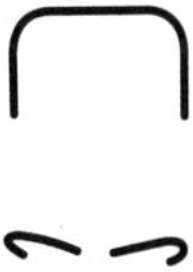

FOR SUE, CHRIS, BEN & SALLY

CONTENTS

10.

INTRODUCTION
BY LUC SANTE

Consider the spot illustration, the unsung toiler of the magazine page. It is small; it does not call attention to itself; it is missed by many insistent readers as they chase the progress of a story across columns and ads. It is kin to the textual space filler at the bottom of a page, but its language is visual, so it is there to make a spark as well as to balance out column inches. No publication has been quite as loyal to the spot as *The New Yorker*, which since 1925 has—with sundry accommodations to changing times—remained attached to a formal magazine-design language with roots in the nineteenth century, when text ruled. In the past, *The New*

Yorker's spot drawings were fairly random, with different artists slinging contrasting styles and themes within a given issue. You got the impression the art department organized and deployed spots primarily by size. In recent decades, though, the magazine has made a practice of assigning all the spots in an issue to a single artist. That, in addition to the fact that digital composition has largely eliminated the physical need for spots, has given the spot a new job. Now *The New Yorker*'s spot is no longer a stopgap but an attraction in its own right—even if its inherent modesty has thus far kept it a cult favorite.

It shouldn't come as much of a surprise that the protean Richard McGuire has been quietly reveling in the form. McGuire, who wrote and drew the ineffable, time-traveling *Here* (2014) and is also an animator, author and illustrator of children's books, maker of toys, creator of singularly memorable covers for *The New Yorker*, and indelible bass player (with Liquid Liquid), looms very large in the comics world while slaloming along a career path that hardly resembles those of any of his colleagues. He is the form's Duchamp—a conceptualist with formidable skills who is disinclined to keep to any one routine but whose every move would make a lifetime shtick for any lesser being. He sometimes employs the spot sequence as if he had been handed a seven-panel strip in the *Daily Bugle* with no restrictions except a ban on words, sometimes as if he were putting up Burma-Shave signs along a highway, sometimes as if he were unveiling sample frames from a flip-book animation.

Besides the nonverbal nature of the spot sequence, and its limits on size and detail, the other primary consideration of the form is spatial: the individual drawings are widely separated, pages apart, so each spot must be able to stand alone convincingly. Unless you are unusually attentive to spot illustrations, chances are that you will pick up a sequence somewhere in the middle and have to leaf backward and then forward again to appreciate its movement. Sometimes it doesn't matter when you come in, though. Some of McGuire's sequences are taxonomies: bird cages, hats, ice, or the collection of wire shapes that decorates the front matter of this book. They manage to be at once witty and somehow scientific, and you might wish there were a hundred examples rather than just seven. Some of the sequences, like medieval accounts of the lives of saints, are episodic chronicles that can be randomly shuffled, such as the selected investigations of a pigeon, or vagaries in the daily grind of dinner table stalwarts salt, pepper, ketchup, and mustard.

Very often, however, his sequences are narrative, but that aspect has many nuances. They can resemble comic strips, such as the slapstick tale of the flamingo and its umbrella, although the spatial peculiarity of the spot sequence is that time can be approached with a good deal more elasticity than it could in a comic strip. The intervals between individual spots in a sequence can be measured in minutes ("Taxi"), or hours ("MountainCloudTreeFlagManSun"), or weeks, even months ("Three Friends"). A narrative can be loosely connected ("Waves") or tightly plotted ("Spider") or grandly, operatically overdetermined ("Knife, Fork, Spoon; Love Triangle"). It can, for that matter, be strung together like beads on a chain, such as his improbable parody, rich in character and incident, of a famous Norman Rockwell *Saturday Evening Post* cover ("Gossiping Objects").

McGuire has a special gift for endowing inanimate objects with personalities. He accomplishes this with the most minimal means. The hapless parking meter in "Three Friends" has something like a face, set in a permanent cry of affront, and its stolid neighbor the mailbox seems to wear a stiff grin thanks to its handle, but his other objects are animated purely by, as it were, body language. In "Gossiping Objects" the razor's bent neck identifies it as a busybody, while the scissors look gullible—finger loops becoming googly eyes—the toothbrush laughs with its bristles, the toothpaste tube wears a rube's forelock of dangling extruded paste, and the dental floss just plain flies out of control. Those items are all depicted with the strictest realism, without even need for the arms and legs the rock sprouts in "Rock, Paper, Scissors".

He has particularly absorbed classical modernism and repointed it for his own uses. It doesn't take much squinting to see Fernand Léger in "Subway," or Joan Miró in "Taxi," or El Lissitzky in "Sharing Thoughts," or Vladimir Tatlin in "Architecture," or any number of German Expressionists in "Noise Upstairs." Every sequence involves a determining style and one or more formal constraints: bisected faces, a horizontal split, a stretched and twisted grid—or maybe, as in "Touched," a film made entirely of close-ups. McGuire is a virtuoso with an army of styles at his command; they are all present here, in highly distilled form.

16.

THREE FRIENDS

18.

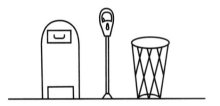

20.

22.

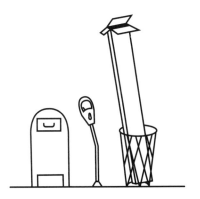

24.

26.

28.

30.

32.

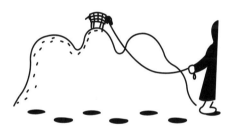

34.

36.

38.

40.

42.

THE HALLWAY

44.

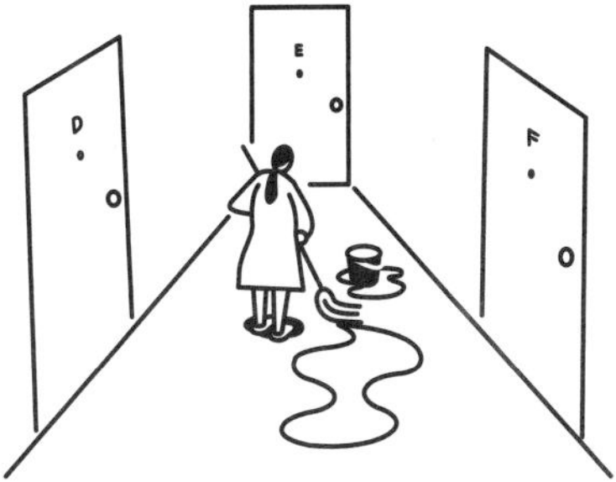

D
E
F

46.

E
D
F

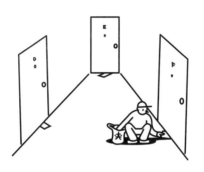

48.

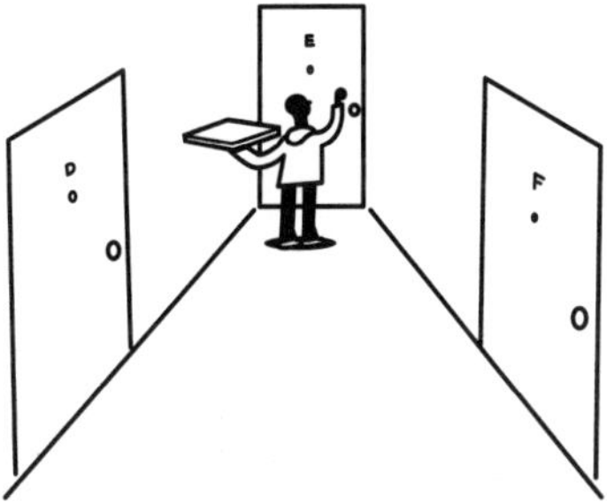
D
E
F

50.

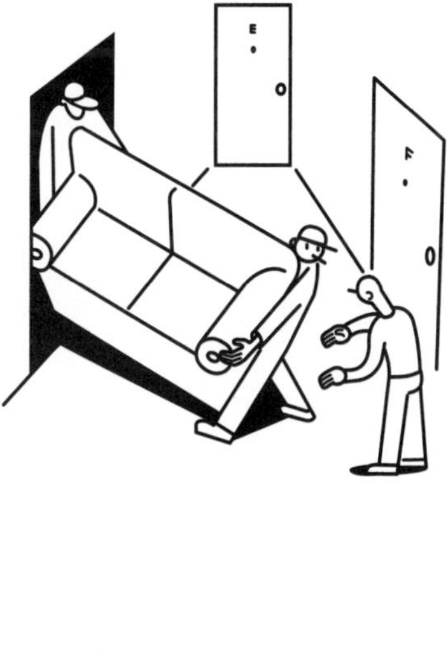
E
F

52.

D
E
F

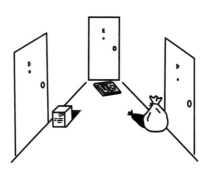

54.

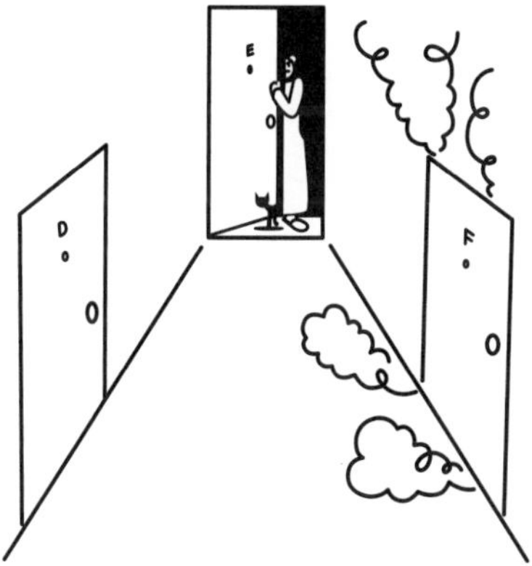
E
D
F

56.

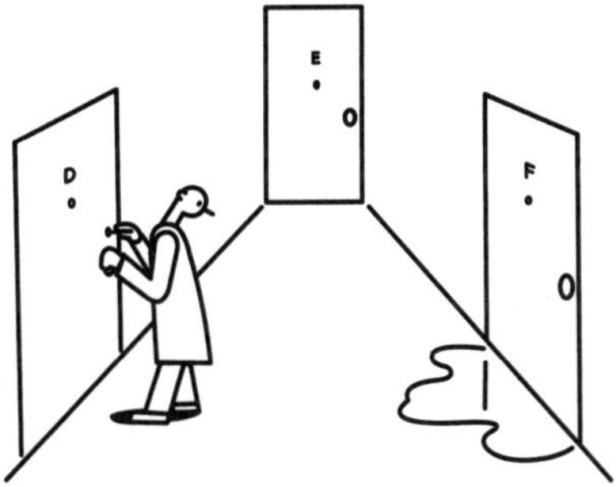
D
E
F

58.

E
F

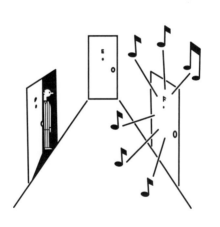

60.

E
D
F

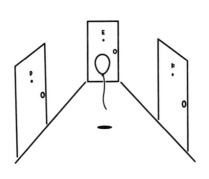

62.

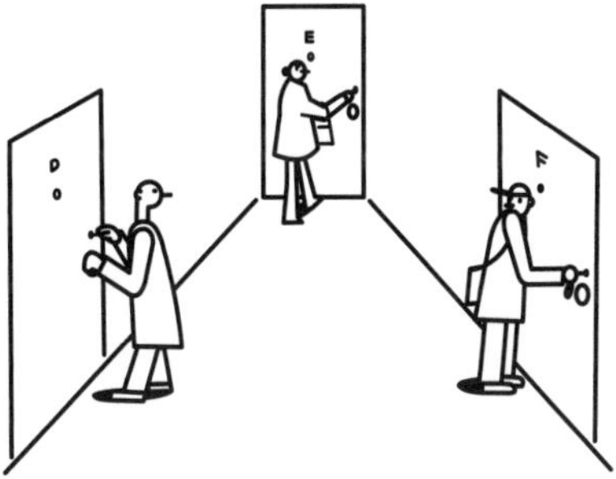
D
E
F

64.

FRAMED

66.

68.

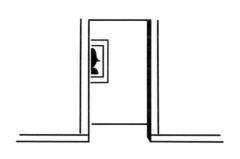

70.

72.

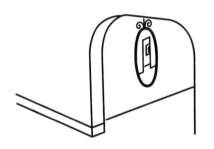

74.

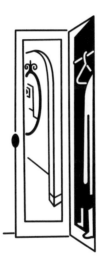

76.

78.

80.

82.

84.

SCENES FROM A TABLE

86.

88.

90.

92.

94.

96.

98.

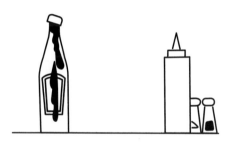

100.

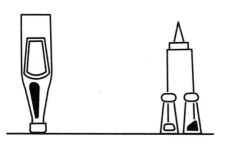

102.

104.

SUBWAY

106.

108.

110.

112.

114.

116.

118.

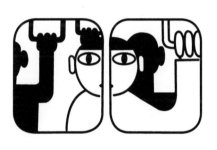

120.

122.

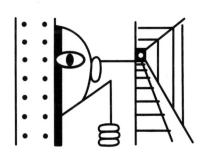

124.

ROCK, PAPER, SCISSORS

126.

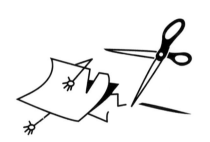

128.

130.

132.

134.

136.

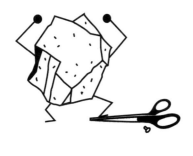

138.

140.

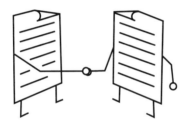

142.

144.

BIRD CAGES

146.

148.

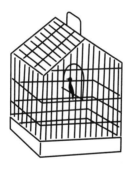

150.

152.

154.

156.

158.

160.

162.

ARCHITECTURE

164.

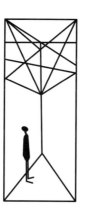

166.

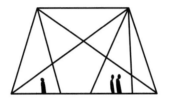

168.

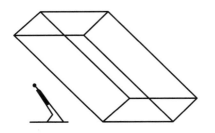

170.

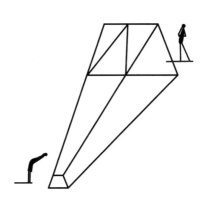

172.

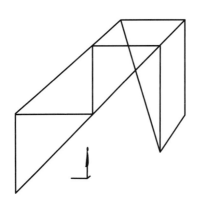

174.

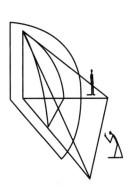

176.

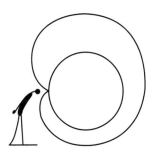

178.

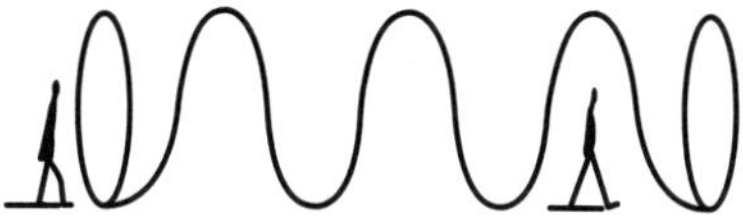

180.

HATS

182.

184.

186.

188.

190.

192.

194.

196.

198.

FLAMINGO UMBRELLA

200.

202.

204.

206.

208.

210.

212.

214.

216.

218.

220.

222.

224.

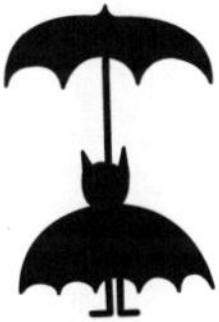

226.

228.

ELEVATOR LOVE

230.

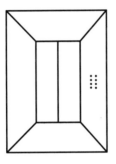

232.

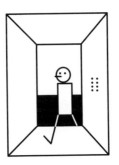

234.

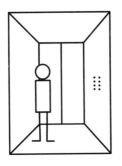

236.

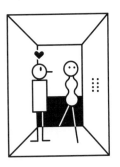

238.

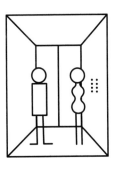

240.

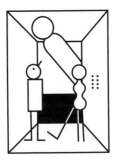

242.

244.

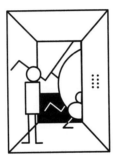

246.

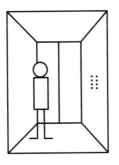

248.

KNIFE, FORK, SPOON; LOVE TRIANGLE

250.

252.

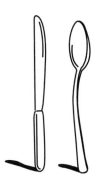

254.

256.

258.

260.

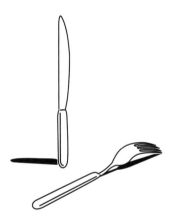

262.

264.

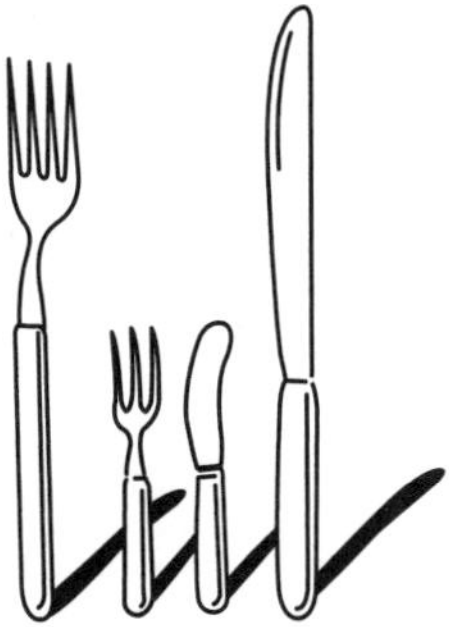

266.

268.

TOUCHED

270.

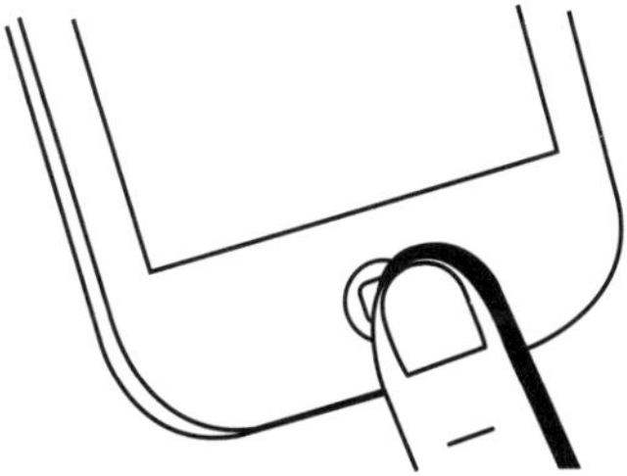

272.

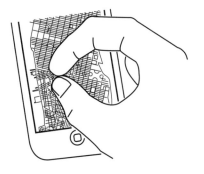

274.

A

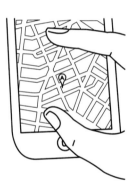

276.

2B
2C
2D
2E

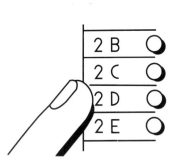

278.

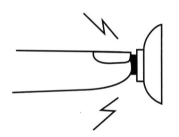

280.

282.

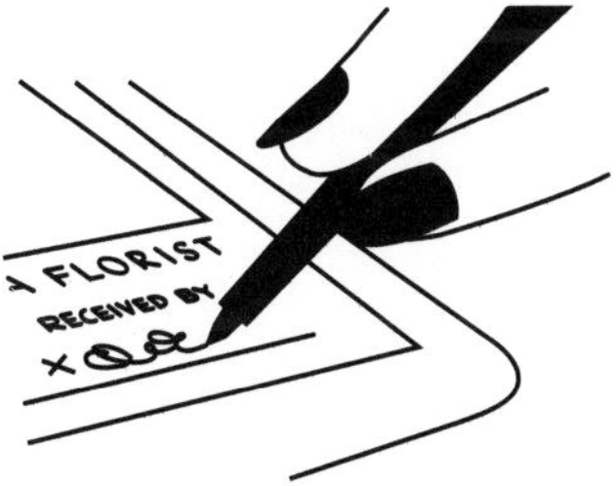
A FLORIST
RECEIVED BY
X

284.

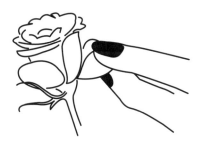

286.

288.

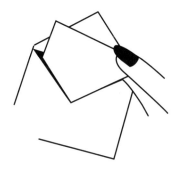

290.

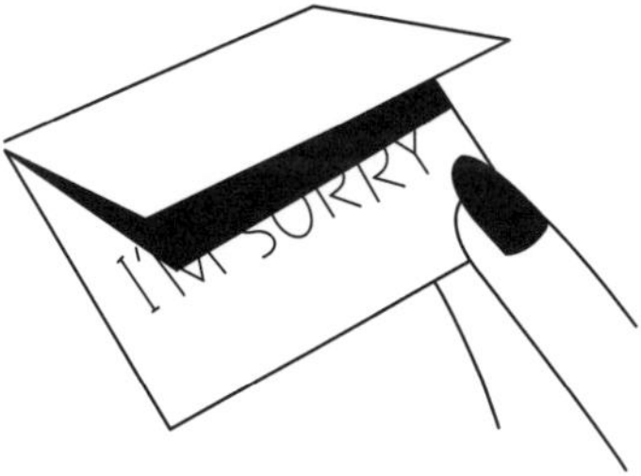
I'M SORRY

292.

294.

296.

shift

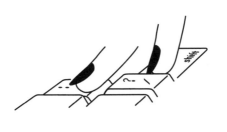

298.

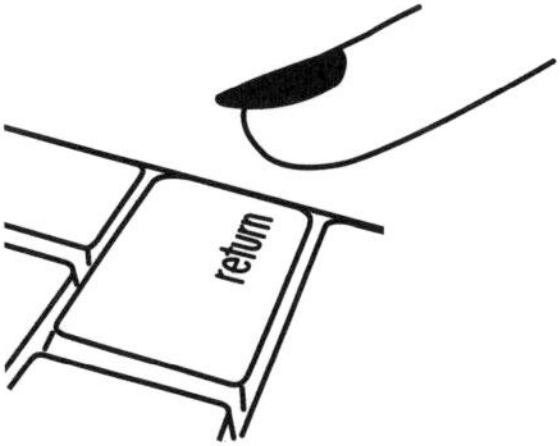
return

300.

NOISE UPSTAIRS

302.

304.

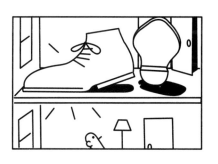

306.

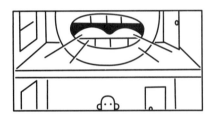

308.

310.

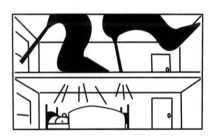

312.

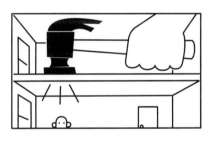

314.

316.

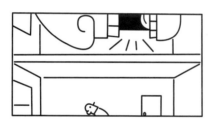

318.

SHARING THOUGHTS

320.

322.

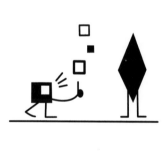

324.

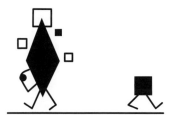

326.

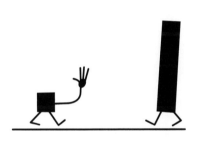

328.

330.

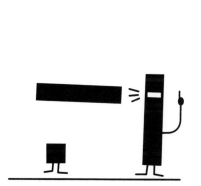

332.

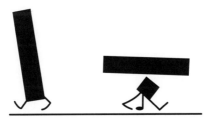

334.

336.

338.

340.

PIGEON

342.

344.

346.

348.

350.

352.

354.

356.

358.

TAXI

360.

362.

364.

366.

368.

370.

372.

374.

ICE

376.

378.

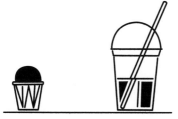

380.

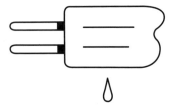

382.

384.

386.

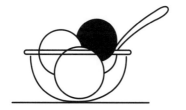

388.

390.

WINDOWS

392.

394.

396.

398.

400.

402.

404.

SPIDER

406.

408.

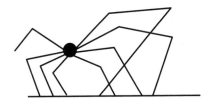

410.

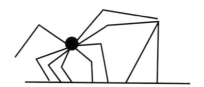

412.

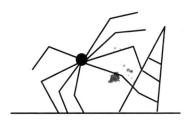

414.

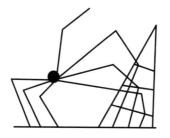

416.

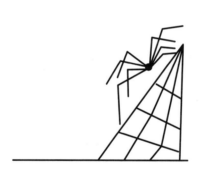

418.

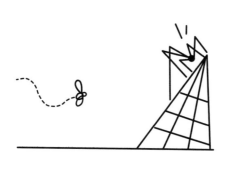

420.

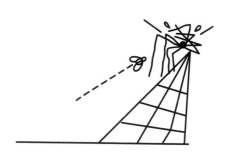

422.

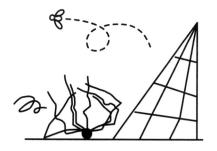

424.

WAVES

426.

428.

430.

432.

434.

436.

438.

440.

442.

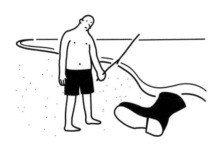

444.

GOSSIPING OBJECTS

446.

448.

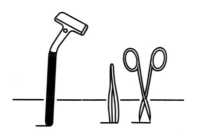

450.

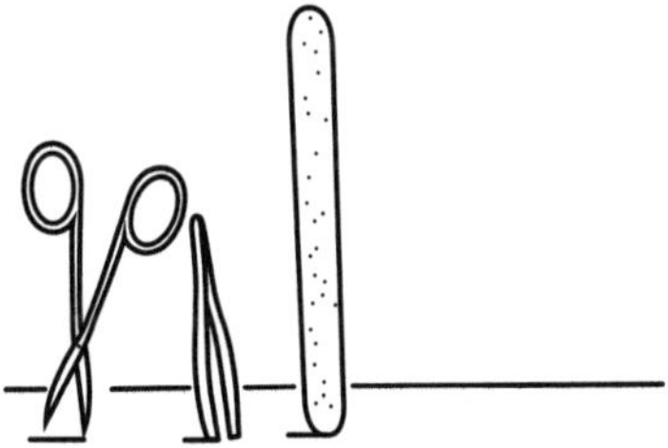

452.

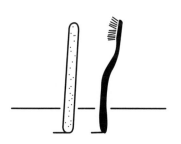

454.

456.

458.

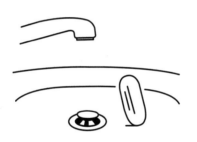

460.

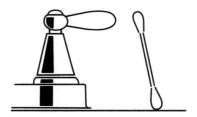

462.

464.

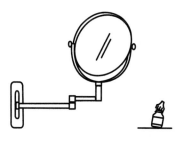

466.

468.

470.

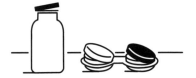

472.

474.

476.

TOURING

478.

480.

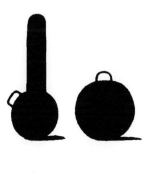

482.

484.

486.

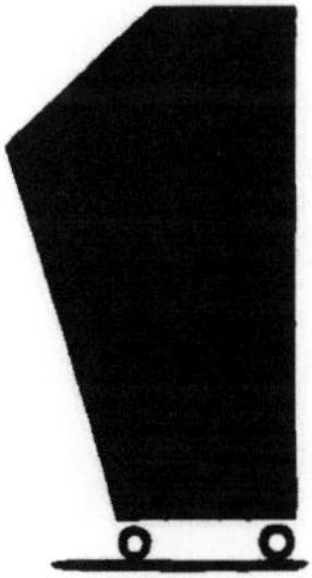

488.

490.

INSECT FASHION

492.

494.

496.

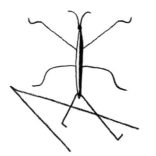

498.

500.

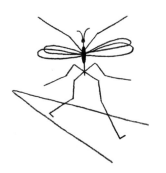

502.

504.

506.

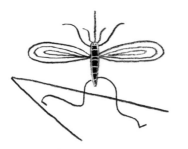

508.

510.

MOUNTAINCLOUDTREEFLAGMANSUN

512.

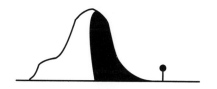

514.

516.

518.

520.

522.

524.

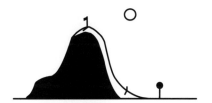

526.

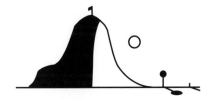

528.

530.

TREE

532.

534.

536.

538.

540.

542.

544.

546.

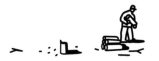

548.

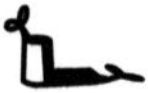

550.

BURDEN

552.

554.

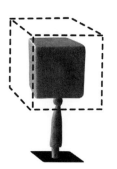

556.

558.

560.

562.

564.

566.

568.

570.

BIRTH

572.

574.

576.

578.

580.

582.

584.